TRAIN

S[T]

TRAINING YOUR STAFF

by Winifred Gode

The Industrial Society

First published 1972 by
The Industrial Society
Robert Hyde House
48 Bryanston Square
London W1H 7LN
Telephone 071-262 2401

Second edition, 1989
Reprinted May 1990
© *The Industrial Society, 1972, 1989*

ISBN 0 85290 436 3

British Library Cataloguing in Publication Data
Gode, Winifred
    Training your staff. — 2nd ed.
    1 Great Britain. Personnel. Training
    I. Title II. Series
    658.3'124'0941·

Typeset by Senator Graphics, London
Printed and bound in Great Britain by Belmont Press, Northampton

CONTENTS

FOREWORD

Whatever the discipline or level of management, the responsibilities of a manager are many and various. It is their job to produce results with essentially just two resources — people and time.

To maximise the potential of both, most managers need some reminders and basic guidelines to help them.

The Notes for Managers series provides succinct yet comprehensive coverage of key management issues and skills. The short time it takes to read each title will pay dividends in terms of utilising one of those key resources — people.

People, though often described as 'the manager's most valuable resource', are rarely seen in terms of investment and return. One of the most effective ways of investing in human resources is to train people in order to improve their performance in their job.

This booklet gives the manager a summary of the various means of training available, together with guidance about how and when to use them. The aim is to ensure that managers choose the type of training best suited to their needs.

ALISTAIR GRAHAM
Director, The Industrial Society

1

WHY TRAIN?

Training is a means of equipping employees to perform competently in their present or future jobs so as to increase the efficiency of the organisation and their own job satisfaction. It is the *planned* provision of the means of learning on the job or in a training centre. The benefits training can give include the following:

- *Reduction of learning time and cost.* People learn the job quickly, to required standards, safely, and with minimum waste of materials or damage to equipment.
- *Improved job performance.* Increased output, improved quality, work done on time.
- *Less supervision* through reduction of problems such as absenteeism, lateness, accidents.
- *Better recruitment and selection.* Training opportunities help attract right type of employees.
- *Reduced labour turnover* by developing employees' potential and their job satisfaction.
- *Reduced costs* resulting from above benefits.
- *Increased customer satisfaction* through improved goods and services.

Training is a line management responsibility from the top executive to the first line supervisor. Those responsible for the successful accomplishment of the work are also responsible for maintaining the effectiveness of the employees undertaking that work.

This booklet aims to acquaint managers with the main methods involved in training and give them some guidance as to when and how they can be used.

2

WHO IS TO BE TRAINED?

New entrants

School-leavers and graduates are unlikely to have any knowledge
or experience either of the type of work done, or of the conditions
under which it is carried out. Adults may have previous work
experience, though not necessarily of the kind they are about to
undertake, nor in the particular organisation.

All new employees therefore require *induction* training in order
to familiarise them with the organisation, its products/services, its
personnel policies, and practices. Some part of this training may
be carried out by the personnel department. But it is the
responsibility of the manager to introduce newcomers to the
department, to train them from the start in the way the department
is run and the standards of performance and behaviour expected
from them.

The importance of induction cannot be over-emphasised,
especially where young employees are concerned. They are at an
impressionable stage in their development, when attitudes to
work can be influenced to an extent which may last a lifetime.
Failure by the manager to give the necessary time and attention to
this aspect of training can result in high staff turnover during the
first few months; poor time-keeping and absenteeism; and a
general lack of interest in the work and commitment to the
organisation (*see* Appendix 1).

New employees seldom bring to the job the full range of
knowledge and skills required. In addition to induction, they must
therefore be trained in the necessary *job knowledge and skills*. The
selection procedure, whereby the applicant is matched against
the requirements of the job, should have shown the gaps which
training needs to fill.

2

Employees needing improvement in present job

If performance standards are to be maintained, it is essential that employees are *appraised* regularly so that any weaknesses, whether owing to deficiencies in the employees themselves, or to changes in the job, can be made good. Identification of such training needs is the duty of the manager: no one else is so well placed to do this (see *Appraisal and appraisal interviewing* and *Target setting* in this series).

Employees preparing for promotion

To be successful, every organisation needs to exploit its resources: the most valuable of these is the human resource. Time and money must be invested in training and developing employees to meet future, as well as present, operational needs. Individual employees also require opportunities to develop their latent talents and abilities. 'Talent spotting' is also the manager's responsibility.

Employees needing retraining

An important factor in achieving success, whether as an individual or an organisation, is the ability to recognise and respond to change. Changes in products, technology, markets, legislation and so on, can affect the way jobs are done and may mean that some, if not all, employees must acquire new knowledge and skills. Responsibility for meeting operational changes is a major part of every manager's job: retraining is vital to achieve this.

Employees nearing retirement

In the interests of both the organisation and the employees, it is necessary to decide how to maintain their performance at an adequate standard, how best to utilise the knowledge and experience they have, while at the same time enabling them to 'run down' in preparation for retirement. Some may learn new skills, e.g. as job instructors; or apply their experience to special projects which are necessary, but difficult to fit into the normal routine; some may have to be trained to accept lower-lever jobs for a period prior to retirement.

3

WHAT TRAINING IS TO BE DONE?

In order to train effectively, it is necessary first to decide in some detail what specific knowledge and skills the jobs involve, what the individuals already possess, and what gaps in such knowledge and skills training can fill.

A systematic approach to the identification of training requirements is described briefly below. To undertake such an approach, the manager will probably need to enlist the aid of a specialist, e.g. a training officer, or consultant.

Identification of requirements

Examine the job

Make a preliminary examination of the job to find out what is involved in its satisfactory performance. Managers may well think they already know all the jobs in their departments. But it is worthwhile observing the whole job, and questioning the job holder about the nature of the activities involved in it. This will be of particular importance when training new entrants, since the previous holder of the job may have modified the way the job is done to suit his or her own strengths and weaknesses — such variations may not suit either the new entrant or the manager's requirements.

Describe the job

Prepare a *job description*, i.e. a document stating the job title, where located, job relationships, purpose, activities — or overall objective, main objectives, and performance standards (*see* Appendix 2).

Analyse the training requirements

Examine the main activities given in the job description so as to identify the tasks involved and the knowledge/skills required for their efficient performance. The extent and depth of this examination depends upon the complexity of the job. There are a variety of analytical techniques, of which the job instruction breakdown is the simplest and can be applied to a variety of jobs (*see* Appendix 3).

The work study or method study breakdown and the skills analysis breakdown are more sophisticated techniques usually reserved for more complex operations, and require specialist training and skill on the part of the analyst.

The result of analysis will provide a *job specification*, i.e. a summary of the specific knowledge and skills required, but not necessarily in the order they should be taught (*see* Appendix 4).

Assess individual performance

The process so far has taken no account of the individual who is to do the job. The new entrant's degree of competence to perform the job should have been assessed when he or she was selected. Existing job holders need regular appraisal to determine how they are measuring up to required performance standards, and what training they need to make good their deficiencies or develop their potential. This assessment will give a detailed statement of what the trainee needs to learn, i.e. a *training specification*. In the case of a new entrant with no knowledge of the job, the *job specification* and the *training specification* are the same (see Appendix 5).

Corporate training needs

Identification of training requirements is not related solely to individuals' performance. Managers need to be alert to the training implications, both for their own departments and the organisations as a whole, of such matters as technical developments, new systems and procedures, market forecasts, changes in employment policies and practices, financial results, etc. Such changes may call for a 'one-off' programme to meet a

6

temporary situation or emergency. But if the organisation is to achieve its objectives, there must be a continuous review of manpower resources to ensure their effective use throughout the organisation.

4

HOW TO TRAIN

Not only are managers responsible for training their staff but, in many respects, they are the best people to do the training. They know the jobs, they know their staff, and have a direct interest in their successful performance. But the way training is carried out will depend upon the numbers to be trained, the complexity of the work to be done, the difficulty of the training process, and the facilities at the manager's disposal. Training can be done:

- on-the-job (on-site, desk training), e.g. assignments/projects, coaching, job instruction, job rotation
- off-the-job (in the organisation), e.g. internal courses, programmed instruction, packaged programmes
- off-the-job (outside the organisation), e.g. external courses, special duties, correspondence courses, guided reading, TV and radio programmes.

The training programme

A training programme may employ any one or more of these means e.g. an on-the-job instruction programme for a new packer; an internal course for a group of supervisors with common training needs; a combination of external courses, coaching and counselling by a manager for a former sales representative newly promoted to supervision (*see* Appendices 6 and 7).

Planning the programme

This should contain all the items in the *training specification* and give details of the order in which they should be taught, the methods to be used, instructional staff, location, timetable. In planning the programme it is helpful to ask — and answer — the following questions:

- Who is to be trained — number and type of employee?
- Why are they to be trained — training objectives?
- What should be taught — knowledge and skills?
- How should training be done — methods?
- Who should do the training — instructors?
- When can it be done — length and frequency?
- Where will it be done — location?
- How will it be assessed — evaluation?

Designing the programme

In designing the programme, consideration should be given to the following points.

- *Sequence:* chronological; order of priority; common/related items.
- *Load and pace:* how much information trainees can absorb and how quickly they can learn.
- *Variety:* subject matter, methods.
- *Feedback:* to test learning, e.g. by setting targets, exercises.

Follow-up

If training is to improve job performance, it is essential that the manager gives trainees an early opportunity to practise their newly acquired knowledge and skills in the job. This may be done by a period of practice under supervision, by coaching and counselling, by assignments or projects, by temporary secondment or job rotation.

Whatever means are employed, the manager must continue to check to see how well the information is retained and used, until he or she is satisfied that the trainees can perform their jobs competently on their own.

Methods

The following sections describe the main methods, the purposes for which they can be used, brief guidance on how to use them, and some indication of their advantages and disadvantages.

Assignment/projects

This is a form of exercise which requires trainees to complete a definite task, generally within a time limit. Such tasks should be based on actual problems facing the trainees' department or organisation, e.g. a high accident rate, customer complaints, high staff turnover.

These exercises are used to give trainees practical experience in applying the knowledge and skills learned previously through formal education or training.

Trainees should be given briefs written in clear, specific terms, e.g. 'list the causes of all lost-time accidents which have occurred in the machine shop during the last two years and suggest how these could be prevented in future'. The brief should also include reference to the type and sources of information required.

The amount of guidance given will depend upon the level of competence of trainees and the complexity of the problem, but as much as possible should be left to the trainees to do for themselves. Trainees should produce specific, practical answers which take account of the policies, practices and general constraints of the situation. The results of their efforts should be presented to and be assessed by their boss, and anyone else who may be concerned with the problem — safety officer, maintenance engineer, etc.

The advantages of this method are that: training activities are directly related to the practicalities of the job; it is a simple means of monitoring trainees' progress and evaluating the effectiveness of the training itself; recommendations produced by trainees may be adopted and the 'pay-off' measured in financial terms. *However*, this method can be demanding in terms of the time of a number of senior people. Suitable for individual or group training.

Business exercises (in-tray)

Some problems have to be solved and decisions made by individuals working on their own. One exercise which deals with this is the in-tray. It simulates the working situation by presenting trainees with a number of items such as letters, memos, reports, similar to those which arrive on their own desks. They must deal with these by writing down whatever actions they think appropriate in the circumstances described in the exercise. The results of their efforts are analysed and discussed on the basis of the decisions made.

This exercise can be used to develop skill in: problem-solving; planning use of time; establishing work priorities; written communications, etc.

It can be run in a variety of ways and the time required will vary accordingly. If it is run as a problem-solving exercise it can take several hours, but if it deals with only one aspect it can be done in about an hour.

Like all business games and exercises, it can provide realistic experience of the techniques and skills of the job. *However*, the benefit is realised only if the exercise material selected is relevant to the needs of trainees. Suitable for group training; adaptable for individuals.

Business games

Groups of trainees, each representing an imaginary organisation (or some aspect of it) operate in a defined situation.

There is a wide variety of business games. A common type involves the planning of a plant, staffing it, scheduling a product, assessing the potential market, planning the sales campaign, and running a viable business for a set period of time. During the exercise, decisions made by trainees are evaluated by 'umpires' (or computers). The results of one set of decisions made by trainees influence their next set of decisions, and decisions made by one group affect the results of competing groups.

Business games enable trainees to appreciate which key factors they must observe in order to understand the state of a business. They can also learn such techniques and skills as planning, budgeting, marketing, problem-solving and decision-making. They can also learn to appreciate the interdependence of various functions in an organisation and the importance of teamwork.

Business games require time (anything from one or two hours to several days) and the resources to run them effectively.

They can provide realistic experience of the techniques and skills needed to run an organisation, and trainees generally become very interested and involved. *However*, 'playing games' may overshadow the learning experience and too much reduction of the time-span in the situation results in superficial learning. Suitable for group training.

The case study method

A case study is a record of a real situation, including the surrounding facts, opinions and prejudices, given to trainees to analyse and discuss. It may deal with one event (e.g. the launching of a new sales campaign), or with a situation involving a number of events (e.g. a strike arising from proposed redundancies following a merger). It may be presented in writing, orally, on film, filmstrip, or slides.

It can be used to teach such subjects as administration, sales, industrial relations, human relations. It is especially useful in supervisory/management training for dealing with such concepts as authority and responsibility. It can also help trainees to develop analytical ability, problem-solving and decision-making skills.

The case study is given to trainees for analysis, discussion and decision as to the type of action which might be taken. In some case studies, however, the action taken is included in the case history: consideration should then be given as to why such action was taken or what alternatives the situation offered. A short, simple case study can be dealt with in 20–30 minutes. Longer, or more complex cases need several hours. If the group is small (five–fifteen) the cases can be discussed by the total group; if larger, trainees may be divided into syndicates, each discussing the whole case simultaneously, or each dealing with a different aspect, and reconvening for a summary session.

In conducting a case discussion, the leader should encourage trainees to 'project' themselves into the situation described so that they deal with it in a responsible way. This is especially important with human relations cases which can develop into a 'witch hunt'.

One advantage of this method is that trainees can draw upon experience and exercise skills which are used in their work without incurring real risk. *However*, unless the cases used are relevant to the needs and interests of trainees, they may be regarded as unworthy of serious attention. In some types of case study, the lack of detailed information about the situation and of a conclusive answer can create a feeling of dissatisfaction on the part of trainees. Suitable for group training.

Coaching

This is a way in which managers can systematically increase the ability and experience of their staff by giving them carefully planned tasks coupled with continuous appraisal and counselling.

Managers should consider the following points:

- *Opportunities* (for coaching) may arise through assessment of an individual's needs for improvement, or through changes in departmental or work procedures.

- *Planning* — agree a coaching plan and timetable with the trainee. Consider: what changes have to be achieved; when have they to be achieved; how will achievement be measured; how will progress be monitored?

- *Assignments* or tasks should be relevant: seek and use suitable work problems. Set high but attainable targets.

- *Monitor progress* — correct if necessary; offer advice, guidance and encouragement.

- *Evaluation* — at the end of the coaching period, review and evaluate the trainee's performance and consider further development plans.

Coaching is a low cost means of improving individual performance and departmental efficiency. *However*, it is only effective if trainees can see its relevance and value to themselves as well as to their work, and the coaching is carried out in a systematic and purposeful manner. Suitable for individual training.

External courses

These are training courses which are organised and directed by an authority other than the trainees' employer. A wide variety of such courses suitable for all types of employees are provided by technical, educational, professional and specialist organisations.

External courses provide opportunities to acquire technical and professional qualifications, training in subjects of which there is no knowledge or experience within the trainees' organisation, and opportunities for broadening individual experience. They are useful for meeting specific individual needs, when numbers are too small for an internal course, or when employees cannot all be released at the same time.

It is important to select the right courses for trainees. Consideration should be given therefore to the following factors:

- type and reputation of the organisation providing the course
- timing — frequency and duration
- location — does it involve travelling time and expense?
- cost — direct/indirect; grant available if any
- the programme — objectives — explicit, realistic
- content — well-balanced, appropriate to trainees' needs
- methods of training — appropriate to content and type of training
- staffing — qualified
- status of course members — comparable level
- facilities and amenities
- administration.

If in doubt on any of these points, the course organisers should be contacted for further information — they generally welcome such enquiries.

A number of bodies maintain advisory services on external courses and will give enquirers assessments of particular courses. Managers or training specialists can also build up their own dossiers on courses which have been found suitable for their employees.

In some circumstances it is possible to liaise with a local technical or commercial college, or other training agency, and get them to organise the particular type of course required.

If trainees are to benefit from external courses, they must be briefed beforehand as to why they are attending and what they are expected to get out of it, and after the course they should discuss the application of their newly acquired knowledge and skills with their boss so that further training or experience may be given. One way of ensuring that what has been learned is put into practical effect is by giving trainees project work. This can also be used as a means of evaluating the effectiveness of the training courses.

Among the advantages of external courses are that they are ready-made, quick and easy to arrange, offer a wider choice of training facilities than can be provided internally, and give trainees the benefit of meeting people outside their own organisation with different ideas and experience. *However*, the disadvantage is that courses catering for a wide variety of trainees tend to be generalised, and the right course may not be available at the right time. Suitable for individuals or groups.

Group discussion

This is an interchange of ideas and experience among the participants, who are guided to achieve the training objectives.

Group discussion can be used to give trainees an opportunity to learn from the knowledge and experience of others, or to promote changes in opinions, attitudes, behaviour. It is a technique which can only be used where relevant knowledge and experience exist within the group, e.g. through prior experience, or can be supplied in a lecture, film or demonstration. The size of the group must be limited: five–fifteen should enable all to take an active part.

To ensure that all trainees benefit from the time spent in discussion, discussion leaders must prepare a plan. They should:

- analyse the subject and decide which aspects should or can be covered in the time available, e.g. 20–60 minutes
- break down the subject matter into manageable steps
- prepare an introductory statement which: defines the subject; explains the discussion plan; and Includes an opening question to get discussion started.

In conducting the discussion, the leader needs to keep the objectives clearly in mind and periodically focus the group's attention on them. Control of the discussion depends mainly upon the guidance exercised by the leader.

The leader's functions are:

- to listen

- ask questions
- clarify misunderstandings
- correct errors
- reject irrelevances
- co-ordinate ideas
- evaluate members' contributions
- give information if necessary
- give interim summaries
- summarise final conclusions.

The advantages of the discussion method are that it gets trainees involved and committed; provides for cross-fertilisation of ideas and experience; gives trainees an opportunity to examine and test their own ideas, attitudes or behaviour and to change them. *However*, unless it is well prepared and conducted it can produce confused thinking and frustration. Suitable for group training.

The incident method

A variation of the case study method, the case consists of a short statement of an incident which has actually taken place. For example: 'The chargehand found two operators fighting. One operator fell against a nearby machine and injured his hand. The chargehand reported the incident to the foreman.' Trainees have to search for the rest of the information by questioning the discussion leader before proceeding to discuss the problem and deciding what action should be taken.

This method aims especially to inculcate in trainees the habit of asking questions and getting relevant information before determining the issues to be resolved and making decisions.

In this type of case discussion, the leader only supplies the information asked for and should allow trainees to come to a decision with insufficient information if they so choose. Their mistakes will become self-evident when they have to justify their proposed actions. As these 'incidents' have actually happened, the action taken by the people concerned is known and can be compared with the action proposed by the trainees. ('Incidents' from the discussion leader's or trainees' own experience are a useful source of material for this exercise.)

Among the advantages of this method are that it: gives trainees practice in obtaining and assessing information; provides an answer to the problem posed and thus overcomes the dissatisfaction which can arise from some case studies. When trainees are organised in syndicates the competitive element can increase involvement. *However*, unless the discussion is carefully handled, there is a risk that trainees attach more importance to getting the 'right answer' than to learning the requisite skills, and also that the group is divided into 'winners' and 'losers'. Suitable for group training.

Internal courses

These are courses for which the organisation and direction of the sessions is the responsibility of the employer of the trainee.

Such courses may be organised and conducted by managers for groups of employees in their own departments, by the organisation's training specialist, or with the assistance of an outside agency such as a technical or commercial college, consultant, etc. However, the involvement of members of management is essential to the success of such courses. Not only are they able to pass on some of their knowledge and experience to the trainees, but the courses give them an opportunity to get to know what the trainees are doing and thinking about their own jobs. The feedback can provide some useful information regarding methods, equipment, products, policies, and may also indicate further training needs.

Internal courses serve to meet training requirements where a group of trainees have common needs e.g. a number of new entrants needing induction or basic job instruction; or when some operational change, such as the introduction of computers, means that a section of employees require retraining, or when there is an overall need, e.g. for a general improvement in supervisory performance.

The advantages of internal courses are that: they are 'tailor made' to meet specific needs, so that issues are dealt with in terms of the organisation's own policies and practices; a body of knowledge and skills is developed which is generally recognised and applied, i.e. a common language and way of doing things; where trainees are drawn from different units, they can get to know and understand one another and acquire a sense of identity; courses can be arranged when required and at a convenient place.

However, unless care is taken to include some sessions which inject new ideas there is a danger of 'in-breeding'. Suitable for group training.

Job instruction

A systematic four-step plan of instruction. Mainly used for training in manual tasks, it can also be adapted for training in procedures and systems.

Prior to instructing, it is necessary to: break down the job into stages; list the operations or instructions which have to be carried out to perform each stage; note the key points (e.g. safety factors, special points of difficulty, variations from normal procedure) which must be emphasised; and prepare the instruction plan, materials and aids.

Instruction plan:

1 *Prepare the trainee* — put at ease; create interest in learning; check existing knowledge
2 *Present* — tell (explain), show (demonstrate) as appropriate, one step at a time; stress 'key points'; instruct clearly and completely, and at a pace trainees can absorb
3 *Practice and test* — get the trainee to do the job or explain the subject; correct errors; check understanding; continue until he or she reaches required standard
4 *Follow up* — put to work; check as necessary.

The advantages of this approach are that it is a simple, economical, and efficient method of job training. *However*, it is less effective where the knowledge/skill requirements are complex. Suitable for individual training; adaptable to small groups.

Job rotation

A form of accelerated experience in the normal working situation aimed at developing existing knowledge and skills or acquiring new experiences.

Trainees are moved for short periods to new jobs. They must be briefed as to what they are expected to learn, and their progress checked to ensure that they benefit from the experience. The amount of responsibility trainees can be given initially must be judged by the extent and relevance of their previous experience. It is also important that the jobs involved are selected for the training and development opportunities they provide and not as a convenient means of filling temporary vacancies. Certain jobs can be reserved as training positions.

This method enables trainees to acquire the specific practical experience they need quickly, instead of having to wait for opportunities to occur through promotions and transfers. *However*, it can be difficult to ensure that the right jobs are available at the right time, and this practice of using or reserving specific jobs for training purposes can sometimes block normal promotion prospects for others. Suitable for individual training.

The lecture

A straight talk without group participation other than through questions at the end. Lectures can be used to give new information, introduce or summarise another piece of instruction, present a case for discussion. Good lecturers are 'masters of their subject and servants of their audience'. Lecturers should:

- define clearly and keep in mind who the listeners are, and what they should know by the end of the session
- check what knowledge they already possess; consider how the subject touches their interests
- decide priorities — what they must know, should know, would like to know
- consider how much time is available, e.g. 15 – 45 minutes
- plan:
  - introduction — tells the listeners the ground to be covered and defines terms which might confuse
  - main points — arranged in an orderly sequence which helps listeners to follow and understand
  - conclusion — summarises the main points, or highlights an important aspect of the subject, or raises a controversial point to stimulate discussion

- decide whether any visual aids or handouts might help listeners to understand the message more easily.

When presenting a lecture you should:

- get the attention of your listeners, e.g. by making a provocative statement, asking a challenging question, using a visual aid, etc.
- speak clearly, in a conversational manner, looking at your listeners and speaking directly to them
- show enthusiasm for your subject and a genuine interest in your listeners.

The advantage of the lecture is that it can give information quickly to a number of people at the same time. *However*, misunderstandings can arise, as the speaker cannot be sure the information is being assimilated. This disadvantage can be overcome if speakers invite questions or ask questions during the lecture, so that they can adapt their material or approach if necessary. (When a lecture is structured to ensure audience participation it becomes a *lesson*.) Suitable for group training.

Packaged programmes ('training packages')

These are available on a wide variety of subjects: leadership, appraisal, employment legislation, job instruction, problem-solving, staff selection. They generally include a training manual, exercises, audio-visual aids, and assume that the purchaser has (or can hire) the necessary equipment — slide, filmstrip or film projectors, overhead projectors, tape recorders, etc.

Most of them require tuition before they can be used effectively. For example, The Industrial Society's Action-Centred Leadership programme requires managers to first attend an external course, and then work under the guidance of a Society instructor on two in-company courses, before they are recognised as competent to run the programmes by themselves (see *The manager as a leader*, in this series).

These programmes can be very useful to the manager, especially in an organisation without a training specialist, as all the hard work in collecting the material, designing the programme and producing instructional aids has been done.

However, they need careful selection, as attempts at adaptation can result in reducing the effectiveness of the programmes in some cases. The initial cost can be high, but is economically viable where the programme can be used for groups of trainees and the material can be retained and used repeatedly. Suitable mainly for group training.

Programmed instruction

The material to be presented appears in small, carefully sequenced segments (called frames). Each frame elicits a response from the learners who immediately find out whether their response was correct.

Two approaches are generally recognised.

1 Linear programming, in which one frame is so carefully constructed and validated that the learner will almost invariably give the correct response.
2 Intrinsic or Branching Programming, which presents several responses from which the learners select the one they think is correct. If they are correct they are told so, and given data for the next frame. If they are wrong they are given further explanation, then directed back to the previous frame to make another choice.

Programmes can be presented in machine or book form. There is a wide variety of published programmes dealing with subjects suitable for industrial and commercial training.

This method can be used where a number of trainees cannot be spared from their duties simultaneously, or where there are wide differences in knowledge of the subject, or learning ability. But trainees should be brought together periodically to ensure a common understanding of what they have learned and its application to their everyday duties.

Programmed instruction is especially useful as a means of learning factual subjects. *However*, where training is concerned with promoting changes in opinions and `behaviour, or the development of personal skills, it is generally less effective. Suitable for individual training.

Role-playing

A form of 'learning by doing' but in a simulated situation. Trainees are presented with a situation which they have to resolve by acting out the roles of the people involved.

This method helps trainees to recognise their own strengths and weaknesses, increase their appreciation of the differing attitudes and reactions of other people, improve their skill in dealing with people, and learn new techniques. It can be used to train in interviewing, staff selection, staff appraisal, chairmanship, negotiating, instructing, public speaking, selling, etc.

It requires the setting up of a typical work situation (e.g. a sales assistant serving a customer) which trainees handle as they think appropriate, or behave as they think people who normally find themselves in such situations would behave. Their performance is observed and discussed by the trainer and the rest of the group. Role-playing can be combined with other methods, such as, for example, a lecture on the principles of selling followed by role-play exercises in which trainees apply these principles in dealing with customers; or a case study discussion concerning a disciplinary problem which may be resolved by the trainees 'acting out' the roles of boss and subordinate.

Role-playing is a method which should be approached with care; success depending to a large extent upon the trainer's ability to create a friendly, permissive atmosphere in which trainees feel able to act out their roles and to take and give criticism. It is best done with smaller groups (six–eight) so the trainer can control the whole exercise; larger groups can be divided into syndicates composed of role-players and observers. Time must be allowed for briefing trainees, doing the role-play and discussing it — a minimum of 30 minutes, generally longer.

An advantage of this method is that trainees can practise skills and experiment in behaviour while protected from the real consequences of their mistakes. *However*, it can expose the sensitive trainee to destructive criticism, or create difficulties in personal relationships. Suitable for group training.

Special duties

These are specific tasks assigned to trainees which will enable them to acquire experience outside their normal job duties.

Such activities might include representing the organisation on external bodies, membership of a professional/technical body, technical teaching, youth club leadership, secondment to agents or subsidiaries, attendance to trade exhibitions, and so on.

These tasks should be carefully selected and assigned at relevant stages in the training programme. They can provide useful experience — especially for employees in line for supervisory or management jobs. *However*, they may involve absence from normal job duties, and must be planned accordingly. Suitable for individual training.

Miscellaneous methods

Correspondence courses, guided reading, TV and radio programmes, can all provide a means of acquiring knowledge and skills applicable to a variety of jobs. Like all methods they must be selected carefully. Some guidance must be given to the trainees as to how they should deal with the material; specific arrangements made for the reading, viewing etc. to be followed by individual or group discussion; and some tests (oral, written, or practical) devised to assess what has been learned. Suitable for individual or group training.

5

EVALUATION

Time and money spent on training is only justified if the training contributes to the efficiency of the organisation and improves the performance and prospects of employees. Evaluation — the assessment of the total value of any training activity — is therefore essential.

Managers are well placed to do this. Through the methods described in Chapter 3, managers can identify the lack of the knowledge and skill which is needed to do a job to required standards, or those operational problems which training can solve. They can then carry out the training needed. After the training they should reassess the individual's performance or re-examine the problem area, to test what the training has achieved. The manager should ask the following questions.

- Did results meet the training objectives? (E.g. what evidence of improved performance?)
- What benefits accrued to the organisation?
- Were there any spin-offs not directly related to the training objectives?
- What was the cost?
- How will decisions about future training be affected?

In addition to making their own assessments, managers should ask the trainees how they felt they benefited from the training, and get the views of other people who may have been involved, e.g. other managers, supervisors, instructional staff.

Evaluation is comparatively simple in cases like that of new entrants with no previous experience of operating a machine, who after training can demonstrate that they can operate the machine in a safe, efficient manner and produce the required quantity and quality of work. It becomes more difficult with more complex jobs, e.g. supervisory jobs, and in such skills as decision making, where the results of decisions may only be measurable in the long term, and other influences may affect results.

However, although in some cases it may be necessary to accept inconclusive evidence rather than proof, it is still worthwhile evaluating training. Provided the objectives are identified in specific, measurable terms (e.g. to take shorthand dictation at 80 wpm and transcribe it accurately; to reduce errors in invoices, customer complaints; to increase output/sales by so much), it is possible to demonstrate 'cause and effect'.

Training records

Simple records can assist the manager in deciding who needs training and when, and ensure all staff are receiving the required training.

There should be: an *individual* record for each trainee, giving name, department, date of joining, and details of the training — i.e. dates (start and completion), objectives, method, result of training, cost, further action; and a *department* record, giving names of trainees, type of training, dates, results of training, costs, further action.

6

THE TRAINING SPECIALIST

A competent training specialist can help the manager with:

- analysing jobs
- preparing job descriptions
- preparing appraisal systems
- identifying operational problems that training can solve
- planning the training programme
- giving advice on selection of training methods, techniques, aids
- preparing training materials
- implementing the training programme in specific areas delegated by management (e.g. basic skills training) or areas of particular complexity (e.g. group relations training)
- evaluating training
- preparing training budgets
- keeping records
- training managers, supervisors and others in instructional techniques and skills
- keeping managers informed of developments in the training field.

The function of the training specialist is to advise and assist line management to carry out their responsibilities for training and developing their subordinates. He or she is the specialist in training — they are the specialists in running the organisation.

The training specialist may be employed full-time (large organisations may need a training department), or a senior executive can undertake this function as part of his or her regular job. In either case, the training specialist can only operate effectively with the support and active involvement of line management.

APPENDICES

APPENDIX 1

INDUCTION CHECKLIST

Information (organisation)
Name
History
Organisation chart
Products/Services
Customers
Location

Information (departmental)
What it makes or what services it gives
Where it fits into the organisation
Jobs done, trainee's job — where it fits
Departmental rules (time-keeping, meal breaks, safety, smoking, etc)
Supervision — names
Other employees — names
Personal relationships

Employment conditions
Remuneration
Make-up of pay (bonus or other plus rates, deductions)
Method of payment (how, where, when)
Hours of work — overtime, weekends, shifts
Holidays
Sickness payment scheme
Pension scheme
Bonus or profit-sharing
Notice period
Time recording and time-keeping
Absence — notification, certificates, pay

Health, safety, welfare
Medical examination
Medical/first aid facilities
Toilet and cloakroom facilities
Hygiene (personal/process)

Safety (regulations, appliances)
Protective clothing
Fire precaution procedures
Smoking
Canteen facilities
Sports and/or social club
Savings schemes
Purchase facilities
Parking facilities
Travelling arrangements
Telephone calls
Time off
Loans
Personal problems

General
Joint consultation (works/staff advisory committee)
Grievance/disciplinary procedures
Union membership
Education and training
Promotion and transfers
Suggestion scheme
Security arrangements

Note: All this information cannot be given to new employees at once: give them the essential information about *their job* and *their department* first.

APPENDIX 2

EXAMPLE JOB DESCRIPTION

Job title   Secretary
Location   Personnel department
Responsible to Personnel Manager
Relationships   Works in department of six people: personnel officer, secretaries, and clerks. Liaises with all other departments — in particular Wages Department, Time Office, Medical Department, Training Centre.

Overall objective
To assist the department manager by providing an efficient and responsible secretarial service.

Main objectives
1 To deal with correspondence.
2 To arrange for and record proceedings of meetings.
3 To maintain confidential files.
4 To deal with telephone enquiries.
5 To make appointments for manager.
6 To receive callers.
7 To make travel arrangements.
8 To deal with routine matters in manager's absence.
9 To maintain effective communication, internal and external.
10 To keep abreast of developments in the organisation, especially those affecting personnel policies and practices.

Performance standards (part of)
1 ● Receive and sort manager's mail; draw attention to urgent matters.

   ● Take down in shorthand and transcribe accurately all correspondence in accordance with house style (minimum speeds: shorthand 90 wpm, typing 50 wpm).

   ● Type letters, memos, reports, etc. by copying from manuscript or printed documents, to accepted standards of layout, accuracy, speed.

- Deal with routine items of correspondence on own initiative, i.e. such items as are determined by the manager.

- All items of correspondence to be dealt with on day of receipt if possible, but not later than two days after.

2
- Fix date, time and place of meetings in accordance with manager's instruction.

- Prepare and send out notices, agenda, minutes and other items, not later than two clear days beforehand.

- Be in attendance at least 15 minutes before start of meetings to check final arrangements with manager.

- Take shorthand record of proceedings; resolutions and 'action points' to be taken verbatim (shorthand speed 120 wpm).

- Draft minutes and/or reports in accepted format and give to manager for checking not later than 48 hours after meeting.

- Check with manager any follow-up action after meeting.

APPENDIX 3

EXAMPLE JOB INSTRUCTION BREAKDOWN

Divisions of job or tasks: telephone; in-coming calls

Stages	Key points
(What has to be done; main steps/normal procedures)	(How it is to be done; important points, e.g. performance standards, variations, difficulties, safety points)
Pick up receiver	Promptly
Identify self and department	Speak clearly
Ask for or check name, organisation, address, telephone number of caller	Repeat and write down — check spelling
Determine purpose of call	
Decide if you can deal with it	
If so, provide information	Be clear and concise
Record message	Use message pad. State date and time of call; name, organisation, address, telephone number of caller; the message; action taken; initials
Close conversation — recap action	Briefly
If information not at once available arrange to call back	Check when convenient
If unable to deal with call yourself, transfer to appropriate person/department	Ask caller to hold — contact switchboard by dialling on internal telephone — do not 'buzz' external telephone. Check if person available
	Be courteous and helpful throughout

APPENDIX 4

EXAMPLE JOB SPECIFICATION (part of)

Job description	Tasks	Knowledge and skills required
1 Deal with correspondence	Sort mail	Know scope of work of personnel department to identify urgent items.
	Take dictation	Write shorthand: minimum speed 90 wpm
	Transcribe correspondence	Type: minimum speed 50 wpm. Know company's house style. Use of English: spelling, vocabulary, punctuation.
	Copy type from MS or print	Type: minimum speed 50 wpm. Knowledge of layout, tabulating.
	Deal with routine items	Know specific aspects of work of personnel.
	Observe office routines	Knowledge of stationery, duplicating, filing, mailing equipment, facilities, etc.
2 Arrange and record meetings	Arrange meetings	Knowledge of types of meetings, membership facilities. Ability to plan and organise meetings.
	Prepare papers	Skill in drafting notices, agenda, minutes, reports.
	Despatch papers	Knowledge of duplicating and mailing facilities.
	Record proceedings	Knowledge of meeting procedures. Skill in reporting. Shorthand: speed 120 wpm.

APPENDIX 5

EXAMPLE TRAINING SPECIFICATION (part of)

For new entrant who has done GCE 'O' level, secretarial course (shorthand: 100 wpm, typing: 50 wpm), one year's experience as shorthand typist in wages department of associated company.

Knowledge and skills required

- Knowledge of organisation, structure, personnel, products, etc.
- Knowledge of scope of personnel department.
- Knowledge of external contacts.
- Knowledge of specific aspects of work to be dealt with on own initiative.
- Knowledge of office routines: stationery, filing, mailing, duplicating, equipment facilities, etc.
- Knowledge of types of meetings, membership, facilities.
- Ability to plan and organise meetings: fix date, time, book rooms, visual aids, etc.
- Skill in drafting notices, agenda, minutes, reports, etc.
- Skill in reporting.
- Write shorthand at speed of 120 wpm.
  And so on . . .

APPENDIX 6

EXAMPLE INDIVIDUAL TRAINING PROGRAMME
(part of)

Objectives. At the end of this part of your training you should: be familiar with the organisation; know the work of the personnel department; be able to deal competently with the correspondence; be able to type copy to required standard; be competent to arrange meetings and record proceedings; demonstrate a shorthand speed of 120 wpm.

Item	Method	Instructor	Location	Time
Knowledge of the organisation	General induction course	Training Personnel manager	Training centre	½ day
Knowledge of work of personnel department: scope/specific aspects	On-the-job	Manager/deputy	Department	Spread over several weeks
Knowledge of external contacts	On-the-job; visits	Manager	Department	Spread over several weeks
Knowledge of secretarial routines	On-the-job	Senior secretary	Department	Spread over 5 days
Knowledge of meeting arrangements	On-the-job	Manager	Department	2 hours
Knowledge of meeting procedures; skill in reporting, drafting, etc.	External course	Specialist instructor	External centre	1 week
Increase shorthand speed to 120 wpm	Coaching	Specialist instructor	Training centre	1 hour per evening until proficient

EXAMPLE COURSE TRAINING PROGRAMME

Objective. At the end of the training period supervisors should: know the appraisal scheme; be able to assess an employee against a job description; complete appraisal forms and write reports; conduct appraisal interviews.

Subject	Method	Instructor	Time	Aids
First day				
1 Why we are introducing an appraisal scheme — benefits to supervisor and company	Talk and discussion	Senior manager	1 hour	Chart pad
2 The scheme — what it is and how it operates	Talk and discussion	Trainer	1 hour	Slides or transparencies
3 Preparing job descriptions	Talk and questions	Trainer	½ hour	Chart pad Specimen documents
	Practical exercise: preparing job descriptions		1½ hours	
4 Assessing the person	Talk and questions 'Syndicate' discussion	Trainer	½ hour	Case study Chart pad
Second day				
5 Appraisal reports	Talk and questions Individual exercises — filling up forms, writing reports	Trainer	½ hour 1½ hours	Slides or transparencies Specimen forms
6 The appraisal interview; what to do before, during and after	Filmstrip and discussion Role play exercises (two groups); summary session	Trainer Trainer and assistant	1 hour 2½ hours	Sound filmstrip Case studies
7 Action session: how the learning is to be applied	Discussion	Senior manager	½ hour	Action notes Chart pad

Note: The 'trainer' could be the departmental manager, the training/personnel officer, or an outside specialist instructor